TYING
FOAM FLIES

Skip Morris

Illustrations by
Richard Bunse

Photography by
Skip Morris and Brian Rose

Frank Amato
PORTLAND

DEDICATION

He showed me that foam offers vast possibilities to the fly tier.

And even though I wrote this book (and even though this may sound trite), the inspiration for it came from his work. So it is without hesitation (or choice, actually) that I dedicate *Tying Foam Flies* to Richard Bunse.

ACKNOWLEDGMENTS

It's becoming clear to me that one of my duties as a teacher of fly tying (a duty I often neglect) is to sort and judge every bit of fly-tying information I can find. *Tying Foam Flies* is much enhanced thanks to the fine tiers from whom I've gathered information. Those tiers are too many to name here, too many to recall. So I must thank by name only those who contributed directly and within the brief span my memory will contain, but to all who ever shared with me a twist or theory, thank you.

For their fly patterns or fly samples or techniques or knowledge or any combination thereof, I thank the following tiers: Bill Blackstone, John Betts, Richard Bunse, Ken Fujii, Craig Mathews, Rod Robinson, Dave Hughes, and Rick Hafele.

For their help or advice or generosity or patience or any combination of these, I thank the following people: Brian Rose, Ken Mitchell, Frank Amato, Nick Amato, Tony Amato, Cindy Tyree, and (the term "patience" applies here especially) Carol Ann Morris.

©1994 by Skip Morris

ALL RIGHTS RESERVED. No part of this book may be reproduced in any means without the written consent of the publisher, except in the case of brief excerpts in critical reviews and articles.

Published in 1994 by Frank Amato Publications, Inc.
P.O. Box 82112, Portland, Oregon 97282
(503) 653-8108

Softbound ISBN: 1-878175-89-0
Hardbound ISBN: 1-878175-90-4

All photographs taken by author except where noted.

Front and Back Cover photographs: Brian Rose

Book Design: Tony Amato

Printed in HONG KONG

1 3 5 7 9 10 8 6 4 2

TABLE OF CONTENTS

FOREWORD

Today's fly tyers are blessed with a wealth of materials at their fingertips.

Each trip to the fly shop reveals something new to make tying easier: a better hackle, a finer thread, a new dubbing or a flashier tinsel. Rarely does a new material have the potential for revolutionizing fly design and opening the door to innovation that some of the new synthetic foams have.

Only foam has the unique quality that allows it to be crafted into some extraordinarily realistic imitations, imitations that not only look natural but float and feel like a natural.

Several years ago while fishing the McKenzie River with Skip Morris I showed him a new foam pattern I was using to imitate the Western March Brown. Skip is a talented and creative tyer and I could tell by the look in his eye and the light bulb over his head that he could hardly wait to get to a fly tying vise.

Since that trip Skip has gone far beyond that March Brown imitation to develop many ingenious patterns using several types of foam and a variety of tying techniques. He has presented these patterns and techniques in *Tying Foam Flies*. He has also brought together many interesting and creative patterns from tyers throughout the country. Some of these patterns I have used with great success and others I am anxious to try.

Tying with foam opens a myriad of possibilities but it also presents the tyer with some technical difficulties. In this book Skip has clearly defined the tying steps and guides the tyer easily through them.

Tying Foam Flies will be a valuable book for both the beginning tyer and the experienced tyer looking for new ideas. For some it will be the impetus for developing your own patterns using these techniques to solve some of those impossible hatches.

So let your imagination run wild and enjoy the exploration.

—Richard Bunse
May, 1994

INTRODUCTION

Book introductions often begin with something like, "Without Bob, this book could never have been written." (Bob is a sample name; this has been said of people other than Bobs.) I'm usually suspicious about the notion that Bob's absence would have killed the book. Likely this is just a familiar way of saying a deeply sincere thank you. In the case of *Tying Foam Flies*, however, that trite old phrase probably *is* true, but the name isn't Bob; it's Richard Bunse.

Richard was not the first to tie a fly body on a needle (I'd even tried it myself long before I met him), but the *way* he tied that body and blended it into a fly–ingenious. Seeing Richard tie his Bunse Dun was what wound me up about foam flies and finally about writing this book. So as you can see, even a trite old phrase sometimes has meaning.

The best way I can describe Richard is to say that if he were somehow transformed into a dry fly, it would likely be his own Bunse Dun. They have a lot in common–both are unpretentious yet unique and innovative. The big difference is color–the Bunse Dun is usually yellow or green and Richard usually isn't.

My research into foam flies turned up some good ones, but I found surprisingly little in the way of innovation, usually just some variation of the basic foam-beetle approach. The foam-beetle approach is fine, but Richard's approach made it clear that there was, and is, lots of room for exploration. And exploration is what I have been doing for the past few years, trying all sorts of variations with needles, foam sheeting, foam chunks, and every foam-possibility I could imagine. I'm sure that there will be many more foam flies from innovative tiers; nevertheless, the flies described in *Tying Foam Flies* have proved durable, buoyant, and effective. They will serve you honorably. They may even surprise you,

because most foam flies last long, and they float and they float and they float. Besides, they are fun to tie.

But there are tiers other than Richard who influenced *Tying Foam Flies*. I, for one, probably had *some* influence since I wrote it. Rod Robinson's flies with foam-cup cores illuminated a foam-fly twist I've seen nowhere else and which gave *Tying Foam Flies* a dimension it would otherwise have lacked. It was John Goddard's Suspender Hatching Midge that likely inspired others to buoy nymphs with foam; his work and theirs (at least all that I could track down) lies within. John Betts has been a true pioneer of tying with synthetic materials of all kinds, including foam–how could he *not* have been an influence? Foam is making the rounds, keen tiers are recognizing its advantages, and you will undoubtedly see increasing use of it in fly tying. The list of tiers who have found new twists in foam flies continues to grow.

Tying Foam Flies does not cover all the bases. For example, the tying section covers two types of mayfly dun but no mayfly spinner. I cold have offered one fly for each category, but the result would have been a book of neater format and less substance. There are two mayfly duns because each illustrates a fly-tying approach that can be applied to all kinds of patterns. No mayfly-spinner pattern I found would have illuminated a specific approach; it would have been there just to make the book seem complete. If you want a pattern for a mayfly spinner, you will find two of them listed in "Additional Foam Flies," and the tying techniques you will need for them are in the tying section. That's how this book works.

There is plenty more to say about foam flies, but if I've done my job, then what you need to know lies in the pages to come.

—Skip Morris

FOAM TYPES

I see fly-tying foams from the simplest of perspectives–a foam is soft or hard or rigid (or Ethafoam, which stands alone), and it is either open-cell or closed-cell. "Open-cell" describes foam that contains open pockets and therefore absorbs water; "closed-cell" describes foam whose pockets are airtight and, of course, watertight and is therefore buoyant. Only closed-cell foams are dealt with in this book. Beyond this, it's just a matter of whether or not a foam looks or feels or seems right for the job at hand. This is pure pragmatism, but it doesn't allow me to discuss foam in much depth.

Knowing little about the makeup and formation of the foams used in fly tying, I asked for help from my friend Cindy Tyree, who manages Northwest Foam Products Inc., and I contacted John Betts–John is well known as a pioneer in the use of synthetics for tying flies. So here is fly-tying foam from the perspectives of the pragmatist, the dealer, and the pioneer.

SOFT-FOAM

Soft-foam is soft. Clearly, in this paragraph I haven't yet made any statements that could reasonably be challenged. For at least the remainder of it, I'll try to hold to that.

Soft bends and compresses easily. A sheet of soft-foam is limp. Get the idea?

John says that soft-foams (he calls them "flexible") are commonly of three types: polyurethane, vinyl, and polyethylene. Polyurethane foams have the drawback of breaking down under ultraviolet rays–they rot in sunshine. Vinyl foams react to some solvents–they melt when they touch tying glues and cements. But as might be said about Goldilocks (if we may assume she tied flies, and I've seen no evidence to the contrary), "She tried the third one and it was *just* right." John considers polyethylene foam the best of the three for fly tying. It doesn't react to solvents and it holds up well under sunshine. EVA (Ethyl Vinyl Acetate) foam is a polyethylene, Evasote is an EVA, and John's favorite polyethylene foam is Evasote. In other words: John likes Evasote.

John says that EVAs are rigid unless a plasticizer is added during their formation, so rigid, in fact, that EVAs are used to make such things as measuring cups. The amount of added plasticizer largely determines the suppleness of the completed foam. The other factor is the size of the bubbles, or pockets, in the foam–little bubbles leave foam stiff; big bubbles make it soft. These variables–the amount of plasticizer and the size of the bubbles–also explain why there are so many foams that seem nearly identical but differ slightly in feel and appearance.

Most of the soft-foams sold for fly tying are EVAs. Again, they will vary due to plasticizer ratio and bubble size. When you see various names for foams–Evasote, Polycelon, and such–most of those names refer to a specific type of EVA.

I haven't yet found a foam too supple for my taste. I like soft fly-tying materials because I believe that their give helps fish to get past them to the hook. In other words–stiff materials, fewer hooked fish; soft materials, more hooked fish. I'm still looking for a soft-foam that is soft enough.

Soft-foam usually comes in sheets of various thicknesses (unfortunately, not nearly enough thicknesses to suit me, but that can be dealt with as described in section II, "Tying with Foam"). There are also soft-foam cut plugs and soft-foam extruded cylinders. Soft-foam comes in basic white and a slowly increasing variety of colors. Soft-foams are precolored by adding color to the solution before the foam is completed. I have found most soft-foams to be quite durable. Of all the foam types, soft-foam sheeting is the one I reach for first.

A sampling of soft-foams marketed for fly tying. As you can see, even though their colors, thicknesses, and even shapes vary, overall they appear similar.

ETHAFOAM

Ethafoam is an odd one. It's sort of a foam and sort of a puckery cluster-sheet of whitish-clear fine-skinned bubbles. Sort of, anyway. It's durable enough but not as durable as soft-foam. So far as I know, it comes in whitish-clear only. Its best qualities are that it is very supple, its texture and translucence mimic that of some insects, it comes in a very useful range of thicknesses, and it's free. You will often find it used as packing for picture frames, furniture, electronics, fruit, camera equipment, and such.

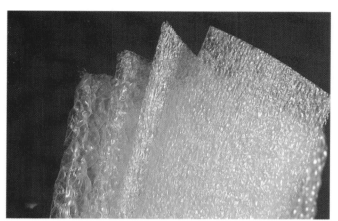
.Ethafoam of various thicknesses.

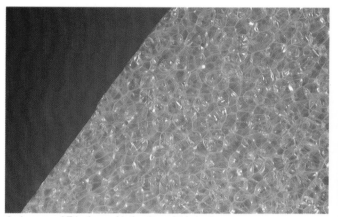
A closeup of Ethafoam. Notice its pebbly texture.

HARD-FOAM

Add only a little plasticizer to an EVA foam and you have (by my definition) a hard-foam (though there may be hard-foams other than EVAs). Hard-foam recovers from flex or compression as well as soft-foam does, but it flexes or compresses quite reluctantly. It's hard—okay?

For certain applications, hard-foams have no substitutes.

Hard-foam on the left, soft-foam on the right. As you can see, they look similar. The big difference (as you might expect) is that soft-foam is soft and hard-foam is hard.

RIGID-FOAM

The only rigid-foam I tie with is expanded polystyrene. Like most people, I assumed it was Styrofoam, and like most people I was wrong. I brought some samples, including a drinking cup and some chunks, to Cindy and she identified them all as expanded polystyrene. Expanded polystyrene is a cluster of tiny white balls. The balls can be worked loose and then used to buoy artificial nymphs. Both sheets and chunks of expanded polystyrene are also useful to the fly tier. These are often cut to shape, secured to a hook, and then covered with some other tying material.

The reason I use the word "rigid" here is because there is very little flex. Hard pressure on expanded polystyrene foam creates an impression–this foam doesn't snap back–and bending a sheet of it very far will break it. This is what I call rigid.

This closeup of expanded polystyrene foam shows its broken edge and a few of the tiny balls from which it is made.

This sheet of expanded polystyrene foam came from a drinking cup— useful and easily obtained stuff for the fly tier.

You will sometimes have a choice of foam type. You may have a choice of soft-foam or Ethafoam, hard-foam or rigid-foam, and even soft-foam or rigid-foam. Generally, such choices aren't critical, but if you choose soft-foam rather than Ethafoam for your Morrisfoam Stone, this *will* determine the way the fly looks, floats, and fishes. Armed with an understanding of foam types and what each is about, you will make informed choices.

TYING WITH FOAM

There is nothing dramatically unusual about tying with foam, but there are peculiarities. What follows is a look at the principles behind tying in harmony with those peculiarities. For more on foam types, see section I, "Foam Types."

THREAD TENSION

Thread-turns over foam compress it, make it denser and from that, less buoyant. Loose turns, however, leave *everything* loose, and loose flies fall apart. The obvious answer is compromise–enough thread tension for soundness and no more. We are primarily talking here of soft-foams, but these principles still have some bearing on hard-foams and rigid-foams.

But there are other answers. Foam colored with a marking pen is often lightly coated with thinned Flexament to secure the coloring, but that cement coating also binds light buoyancy-protecting thread-turns in place. A bit of head cement or epoxy glue strategically added during the tying process is another way to help secure foam to hook.

A closeup of moderately tight thread-turns that segment the abdomen of a Bunse Dun. These turns are lightly coated with Flexament both to secure the color *and* the turns.

Beyond compressing the buoyancy from foam, thread-turns can also cut it–thus tight turns may cut free the very foam they are meant to secure. One cure is to secure the foam tightly, and then work a few snug turns up the foam. The first, tight thread-turns anchor the foam, but should these tight turns cut, the snug turns will hold, giving the fly a second chance at survival. The risk of tight thread-turns cutting foam, as with the problems of tight turns diminishing foam's buoyancy and leaving it poorly secured, can be dealt with by securing the foam with only *snug* turns and adding epoxy sparingly and strategically on hook, thread, foam or all three.

Notice that the foam here is secured with tight thread-turns, but lighter-tension turns work up the foam to protect against cutting.

On the left is soft-foam secured with tight thread-turns; on the right is soft-foam secured with snug thread-turns. The foam on the right might shift on the hook but for a drop of epoxy that was first added to the shank—this drop will hold the foam in place even without tight thread-turns.

COLORING FOAM

Ethafoam that is colored with a permanent marking pen should always be given a coating of thinned Flexament (three parts thinner to one part Flexament). This technique was developed by Richard Bunse. Richard marks the foam with broad strokes of the marker, then lightly brushes out the Flexament. "Lightly" is important here–Richard's brush

Flyfishing Subscription Card

ORDER TODAY!

• Enjoy fly fishing more with a subscription to *Flyfishing* magazine! Each colorful, big issue is packed with information you can use about fly fishing techniques, fly tying, selecting correct flies, casting, reading water, fly tackle and finding the best places to fish. Send this postage-paid card today to start your subscription!

Yes, Please enter my subscription to *Flyfishing* for:

☐ **One Year** (5 issues) **\$15.95**   ☐ **Two Years** (10 issues) **\$29.95**

(Canadian Orders Add \$5.00 per year • Foreign Orders Add \$10.00 per year)

☐ NEW ☐ UPDATE   •   ☐ Check enclosed ☐ Bill Me

Please Charge to My: ☐ VISA ☐ MASTERCARD ☐ AMEX

C.C. No.: _____ Exp. Date:_____

Day Phone:(____) _____

Name: _____

Address: _____

City: _____ State: _____ Zip.: _____

CALL TOLL FREE 1-800-541-9498 (9-5 Pacific Time Mon.-Fri.)

BUSINESS REPLY MAIL

FIRST CLASS MAIL   PERMIT NO. 116   PORTLAND, OREGON

POSTAGE WILL BE PAID BY ADDRESSEE

Flyfishing

FRANK AMATO PUBLICATIONS
PO BOX 82112
PORTLAND OR 97282-9987

merely grazes the high points of the Ethafoam's textured surface. The thinned Flexament spreads quickly.

Brushing thinned Flexament onto marker-colored Ethafoam.

If you are coloring one of the other foams, a thinned coating of Flexament seems to help here too. But I must admit, my experience with this is limited. The ideal is to find a foam already of the proper color, but if you must use a marking pen, at least try to find a foam of a color similar to the pen's. Then if the foam is torn, the underlying color will blend somewhat. The Morrisfoam Predator, for example, can turn from a deadly imitation to a sorry attempt at one if it is tied with just any foam and then colored brown with a marker–a few tears from trout teeth and that dead ringer for a dragonfly nymph erupts with alarming bright-white or bright-yellow spots.

Two Morrisfoam Predators showing the tears that trout teeth can create. The fly on the left was tied with medium-brown foam; the fly on the right with yellow. Both were colored with a dark-brown marking pen. The tears create only a mottling effect on the brown foam, but the yellow breaks out in bright spots. This is an extreme example but, get the idea?

To me, foam that is precolored–colored throughout, not just on its surface–is ideal. As foam flies become more popular, it is likely that foam will come in plenty of useful colors. A foam color that is close can be adjusted to precision with the use of a marking pen–pen color can be blended with foam color to match virtually any insect, and even the markings of the natural can be added. But I'm little concerned with all this because I believe that exact color is rarely criti-

cal to a fly's effectiveness. On my mental list the criteria for a fly's effectiveness, in order of importance, run as follows:

1. *Movement*: whatever the natural insect does (even if it lies motionless), the artificial must do the same.
2. *Size*
3. *Silouette*
4. *Overall Hue*: dark or light.
5. *Color*

I take one through three quite seriously; four I notice; and five I consider a luxury–if I truly match an insect's color in my fly, I get a boost in confidence, but I doubt that the fish notice. Besides, catch a few samples of an insect and you'll likely find that nature is as open-minded about insect color as she is about human skin-tone.

John Betts sees the foam-color issue differently. (If you don't know of John, see section I, "Foam Types" and you'll understand why his opinions bear consideration.) John ties all his foam flies in white. His favorite marking pens are called Design Markers, and with them he can create virtually any color. He brings his pens along fishing and brings flies of white foam. When, say, the adult caddisfly of the moment is determined, John takes out an appropriate-size imitation and then colors it to match the natural. By doing this, John needs only to carry a few "blank" adult caddis imitations of each size rather than a few in each size *and* each color. He can even combine pen colors to match subtle tones (John says to always progress from a light pen to a dark pen if you use two or more; this maintains each pen's proper color). For example, a reasonable range of hook sizes for imitating caddis would be 18 to 8–six sizes. Three flies of each size–eighteen flies. But typical caddis colors include gray, tan, orange, brown, olive, and green–seven colors. Therefore, if John commited his flies to a color beforehand, he would no longer be well prepared with only eighteen flies; he would need one hundred and twenty-six flies. Far cry.

At this writing I am still a fan of precolored foam, partly because I usually find that light or dark is all I need to worry about regarding insect color, which is easy enough to handle, and partly because I don't want to touch up tears in my foam flies. But John's approach makes sense. I can't say that I won't come around to it someday.

A white, "blank," Foam Caddis of Dave Hughes's design and another Foam Caddis commited to a color. The blank could be marked at stream side to whatever color is needed.

SLITTING FOAM

There are, of course, useful foams other than foam sheeting, but I consider sheeting the standard. Ethafoam comes in several useful thicknesses, which is good because Ethafoam loses its buoyancy if slit. But most foam sheeting comes in one thickness, usually about 1/8," so if you need fine sheeting, you must cut it from standard sheeting. It helps to first cut the sheeting into rectangles of appropriate width; slender is easiest. Lay the rectangle flat, on the edge of a flat surface. Pressing down gently against the foam, saw or slide a double-edged or injector razor blade carefully down the length of the rectangle; keep the blade parallel with the face of the rectangle. The result should be two thin rectangles or even three; but this can be trying work and rarely is it accurate, though it is usually adequate. But please remember–*handle the razor blade with extreme caution*. You can make this safer by holding down the foam with something flat and hard, hard enough that the blade won't accidently cut through to your fingers–a popsicle stick, a fingernail file, the edge of an audio-cassette case, whatever.

When precolored foam sheeting, other than Ethafoam, comes in several useful colors and several thicknesses ranging from 1/32" to 1/4," I'll tell my wife to open the champagne.

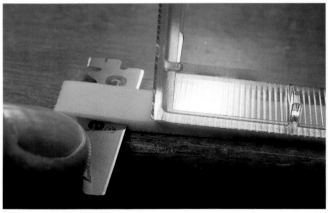

Slitting a foam rectangle.

SHAPING FOAM

Truth is, I generally don't bother with templates for cutting foam–I've tied so many foam flies, at least the ones I fish, that I can make usable cuts by eye. Besides, few foam flies require exact cutting-patterns. But templates can help, especially with unfamiliar flies. You can make the templates from cardboard or any hard sheeting. Cut them out with scissors, tin snips, an artist's knife, whatever. Mark the templates, if you wish, with a fly-pattern name, hook size, hook type, foam size, foam type–whatever helps. You can place the template flat on the foam and cut with a blade, or trace the template and cut the tracings. Most foam flies are tied with simple rectangles of foam, shapes so simple that a template may only slow things. But some foam flies use oddly shaped cutting patterns–a template may really help here. Oddly shaped cutting patterns in this book will have sample drawings.

A Bunse Dun and the template that served to shape its foam body.

SKIP'S WHIP

I used to call this the wet whip finish, but its name has become streamlined: Skip's whip. Skip's whip is very secure because it has head cement all through it.

Many of the foam flies in this book–the Morrisfoam Predator, Morrisfoam Beetle, Morrisfoam Diver, to name a few–are completed with a whip finish that squeezes down into compressed foam–no thread head. For these, the Skip's whip is usually the best and easiest solution.

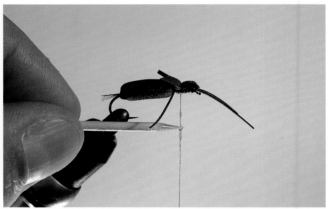

1. To start the Skip's whip, add head cement or epoxy sparingly along 1/4" to 1/2" of the thread near the hook.

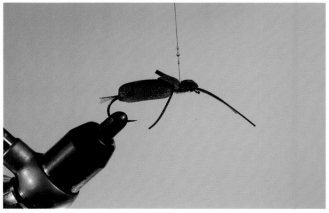

2. Add two to four thread-turns at the whip-finish site.

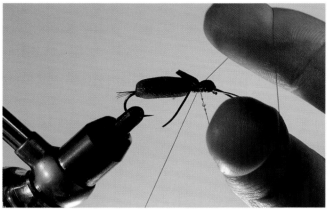

3. Cross the thread over itself in preparation for a whip finish. Cross the thread *near the hook* so that you don't scrape off the cement or epoxy. Whip finish the thread as usual, and then trim it.

THE FLIES

Two Beetles and an Ant

The Foam Beetle has become a new stand-by, and tying it is sheer simplicity. Some think that the Foam Ant's tying is even simpler, but who really cares? Experienced tiers debating this, is akin to chefs debating whether it's easier to boil an egg or warm up canned soup. The point is, tying these two patterns is about as easy as tying gets.

The Morrisfoam Beetle came about soon after my entomologist-fly fisher friend Rick Hafele told me about his Master's thesis. For his thesis, Rick set special traps in a western Oregon creek from early spring to late fall. What he found were a lot of beetles during July and August–great creek-fishing months. This told me that I needed an especially buoyant beetle, since the Foam Beetle simply has too

much hook and too little foam to stay afloat on the tumbling waters of most creeks, at least most of the creeks I fish. The obvious answer was less hook and more foam, and in this case the obvious worked. The Foam Ant is tied in much the same manner as the Morrisfoam Beetle, and in both, the foam-to-hook ratio is easily varied to suit conditions.

So if you are fishing to trout on smooth late-season streams and those trout are focused on ants or beetles, you can use any of the three patterns described here. But if you are fishing lively water, I suggest you tie your Foam Ants with little hook and plenty of foam and for imitating beetles, choose the Morrisfoam Beetle.

Foam Ant

HOOK: Standard dry fly, sizes 20 to 14. (The hook shown is a
   Dai–Riki 305, which is somewhere between a short shank
   and regular shank and can be treated as either.)
THREAD: Black (or a color to match the body) 8/0 or 6/0.
BODY: Black, light red-brown (cinnamon), or red soft-foam.
INDICATOR: Bright-yellow poly yarn.
HACKLE: One dry-fly hackle of a color to match the body.

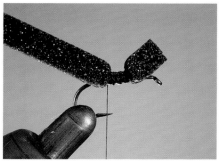

1. Start the thread three-quarters up the shank and wrap the center one-half of the shank with a tight layer of thread. Tie in a strip of foam that is more or less square in cross section, or a foam cylinder, atop the shank at the three-quarters point (I like to smear epoxy along the thread-wrapped shank before securing the foam to it). Secure and compress the foam along the center one-half (or more) of the shank with thread-turns. The front of the foam should project over, and slightly past, the eye.

2. Tie in a section of poly yarn along the thread-compressed foam; the yarn should sweep back over the top of the foam. Trim the yarn closely at its front.

3. Tie in a hackle at the rear of the compressed foam. Advance the thread to the front of the compressed foam, wind the hackle forward in three to five open spirals, thread secure it, trim the hackle's tip.

4. Whip finish the thread and trim its end. Trim the ends of the foam for a short front section and a longer rear section as shown. Trim the poly yarn to a short tuft. Add head cement to the whip finish. You can trim away the hackle fibers underneath and trim the ends of the foam to rounded if you like.

Foam Beetle

HOOK: Standard dry fly, sizes 18 to 8. (The hook shown is a
    Daiichi 1170.)
THREAD: Black 8/0 or 6/0.
LEGS: Black elk hair or fine rubber–strands.
BODY: Black soft–foam strip.
INDICATOR: Bright–yellow poly yarn.

1. Start the thread two-thirds up the shank. Tie in a strip of foam atop the hook (the strip should be about gape wide), and then spiral the thread down the foam and shank to the bend. (If you wish, you can go slightly beyond the bend to create more beetle-body.) Take a few thread-turns at the bend. Trim the stub end of the foam, if necessary.

2. Advance the thread to midshank; there, tie in three to five elk hairs across the shank with crisscrossed thread-turns. The turns should be tight enough to flare the hairs.

3. Advance the thread three-quarters up the shank (some tiers advance it nearly to the eye). Pull the foam forward and down. Hold the foam down under slight tension as you work a couple of thread-turns over it and tighten them. Now you can release the foam.

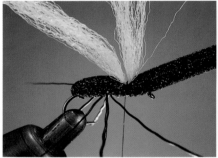

4. Loop a section of bright-yellow poly yarn around the thread, take a turn of thread as you slide the poly-loop into place atop the fly, then pull the yarn back as you take a couple of thread-turns right in front of it.

5. Trim the foam so that it ends over the eye, as a short head. Draw back the yarn and add a Skip's whip (Skip's whip is described in section II, "Tying With Foam") against the front of the yarn. Trim the elk hairs to leg length. Draw up the yarn, and then trim it to a short tuft. (You can trim the foam head so that it appears round from beneath.)

Morrisfoam Beetle

HOOK: Short shank, dry fly, sizes 20 to 10. (The hook shown
   is a Tiemco 921.)
THREAD: Black (brown with the brown body) 8/0, 6/0, or 3/0
   (I'm partial to the 3/0).
BODY: A black (or brown) soft–foam strip.
LEGS: Fine, black rubber–strands (if you can find it, fine
   brown with a brown body).
INDICATOR: Bright–yellow poly yarn.

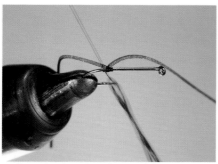

1. Start the thread at the bend. There, loop a short section of fine rubber-strand over the thread, slide it down the thread to one side of the shank, pull the thread tight, and add a couple of thread-turns. Add another length of rubber-strand on the other side of the shank.

2. Advance the thread tightly up two-thirds of the shank, and then add a few tight thread-turns there. Add epoxy glue along the shank, from just behind the eye back to the rubber-strands. The foam strip should be about three-quarters as wide as the shank is long. The front of the foam should project over the eye and beyond it a bit.

3. Tie in a short length of poly yarn atop the foam at the foam's tie-in point. (This is described in detail in caption 4 for the previous fly, the Foam Beetle.)

4. Add a Skip's whip against the front of the yarn. Trim the rear of the foam to square, just past the far edge of the hook's bend. Trim the poly yarn to a short tuft. Trim the rubber-strands to leg length. Trim off the square corners at both ends of the foam.

Foam-Back or Pontoon Nymphs

Nymphs that hang from buoyant foam come in various forms from various tiers. And why not? The concept makes sense; keen tiers would have to see that.

The first foam-back, or "pontoon," nymph I saw was John Goddard's Suspender Hatching Midge. If I could gather the dates on which other pontoon nymphs surfaced I might be able to make a strong argument that Goddard's nymph was the first, at least the first that was well-publicized; but I can't, so I can't. But I'd guess that Goddard's was the first pontoon nymph of any consequence.

In most cases, the pontoon suggests a burst or bursting wing case and the wings escaping it. This tangle of wings and shuck is a messy bulge, and often so is the pontoon; that is why the pontoon is plausible to trout.

This section is not so much about specific pontoon nymphs as it is about the concept of buoyed nymphs–how to make it work, how it can be varied. By approaching

pontoon nymphs in this way, you gain more than just a pattern or two; you gain the knowledge to change other patterns into pontoon flies through several approaches. Why not a Pontoon Gold Ribbed Hare's Ear? a Pontoon Pheasant Tail nymph? even a pontoon soft–hackle fly?

"Why not?" is a blessedly liberating question for the fly tier because it often opens a door somewhere in thought, or at least invites such an opening. It is the question that often rises into thought or speech just before the birth of a new fly pattern or tying twist. "Why not palmer the hackle *back* and then secure it and reinforce it with the rib?" may have preceded the Elk Hair Caddis. "Why not use the wing butts to build a buoyant hump over the abdomen?" may have preceded the Humpy. But of all the "Why not?"s that have flashed along the centuries of fly tying (yes centuries, quite a few in fact), at this moment I am grateful most for the first one that went something like this: "Why not keep a fly afloat by tying it with foam?"

Foam Hump

Hump, fold, stub–whatever it's called and however it's shaped or formed, it is an exposed bulk of foam, near the hook's eye, that buoys the hanging fly. I'll demonstrate a simple, standard approach first; then I'll show you some variations. (Patterns for all the flies shown here are listed in full in section VI, "Additional Foam Flies.")

1. There are more and more suspender flies, especially midge-pupa imitations, featuring a simple stub of foam projecting up or over the eye. The Heathen is used here as an example.

The foam can be tied in first or (as shown here) just before the thorax is formed. In pontoon nymphs of this type, the foam is tipped upwards by tight turns of bare or dubbed thread. The foam can be tied in with its bulk projecting over the eye or (as shown here) over the bend. The advantage of tying it in over the eye is that it is easier to add the tight tip-up turns ahead of the foam than behind it.

2. The Chironomid Suspender Pupa starts as a slim strip of thin Ethafoam tied in about three quarters of the way up the shank. The strip projects off the eye. (The hook shown is a Daiichi 1180.)

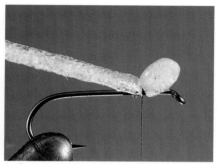

3. Double the foam strip and secure it with thread-turns.

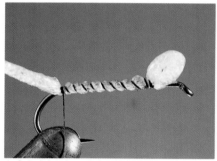

4. Spiral the thread down the foam and shank to the bend—the foam that projects off the bend will be trimmed to form the tail.

5. Some nymphs feature a buoyant foam wing case; the one used as an example here is the Foam Flav Emerger. Complete the shuck and abdomen; then tie in a foam strip at the rear of the thorax area. (The hook shown is a Partridge GRS 3 A.)

6. Tie in the hackle, advance the thread to slightly behind the eye, wind the hackle forward and secure it with thread-turns. Trim the hackle's tip and push the hackle fibers atop the thorax to either side. Draw the foam forward, secure it at the eye with thread-turns, trim the foam closely, build and complete a thread head.

7. For increased buoyancy, push the foam back a bit before securing it at the eye—this will scrunch it up and create a tiny looped wing case with plenty of foam in it.

8. The end of the wing-case foam can instead be trimmed to suggest an insect head, as with the CDC Emerging Midge. (In this case, it is actually a back rather than a wing case, but the principle is the same.)

Foam in Mesh

The foam-in-mesh pontoon is used, most notably, in John Goddard's Suspender Hatching Midge and Charles Brooks's Natant Nymph. It employs a chunk of foam and a patch from a woman's nylon stocking. Both Goddard and Brooks call for a chunk of Ethafoam; but for large pontoons, a chunk of soft-foam or rigid-foam is now the norm, and for small pontoons, a tiny ball of expanded polystyrene (see section I, "Foam Types").

Fly-fishing writers get titilated over the possible approaches to obtaining a woman's nylon stockings for foam-in-mesh pontoon flies. The general idea is that the getting might be more fun than the tying, sort of romancing the socks off the supplier.

I've thought this through and I disagree. In the first place, romancing a woman simply for her stockings is unethical. In the second place, the stocking supplier will almost surely remember what she showed up in and expect to retain ownership of her under things.

So, dull as it may seem, your best bet is probably just to tell a woman-friend that you need some nylon stockings for tying flies, and then work something out. A woman fly tier, of course, needn't worry about any of this, that is beyond some wariness of amorous male tiers of foam-in-mesh pontoon nymphs.

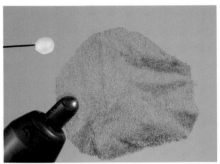

1. Trim a small chunk of soft-foam or Ethafoam to roughly round or (as shown here) work a tiny ball free of some expanded polystyrene. Place the foam in the center of a patch of nylon stocking; then draw the patch around the foam, like a pouch.

2. Tie in the stocking pouch, which contains the foam, somewhere up the shank. Note in the photograph that the mesh is snug around the foam. Trim the ends of the mesh closely at an angle, and then bind the trimmed ends with thread. (The hook shown is an Orvis 1523.)

3. With the pouch tied in, tie the remainder of the fly (in this case, the Suspender Hatching Midge).

Rod's Stones

Rod Robinson's Salmonrod is tied with a core of rigid-foam, and it is the only foam-core fly whose tying we will explore in this book. But it makes a good example for other foam-core flies.

I first wrote about Rod's foam-core golden-stone imitation, a close cousin of the Salmonrod, in *The Art of Tying the Dry Fly*. Though Rod had been tying, refining, and fishing it for years, he'd neglected to name it. I suggested the name "Goldenrod," and Rod relented. So when I later asked him the name of his salmonfly version and he said, "I don't have one," I was not surprised.

This time I asked Rod to think about it and see if he might come up with a name during the following months. He said he would. Several months later I again asked him about a name and he said, "Haven't come up with anything," and again I was not surprised.

By now, I may have made Rod seem incapable of creating a simple fly-name. So in fairness I must tell you that Rod is actually quite sharp. The problem could be that he has some sort of deep kink that makes name-creating terrifically

painful; or it could be that the powers which created him spent all his talent allotment on fly designing, leaving none for fly naming; or it could be that he just hates names. I understand that just before his son was born, Rod was asked what he planned to name the child. Irritated, Rod replied, "The kid'll have a last name—isn't that enough?" There is speculation that had it been left solely to Rod, he would now have the only son in America with no first name. In any case, the name "Salmonrod" is mine, but Rod okayed it.

The Salmonrod differs only in size and color from the Goldenrod; the essential form and tying is the same for both.

Salmonflies are huge stoneflies that hatch from and flutter about western rivers (especially big western rivers) for a few weeks between May and July. Trout sometimes go crazy over them; fishermen always do. A Salmonrod cast around and under streamside cover during this time can be deadly.

A slightly smaller western stonefly, the golden stone, hatches around the same time as does the salmonfly. The golden stonefly is discussed in "The Morrisfoam Stones."

Salmonrod

HOOK: Long shank, dry fly, sizes 6 and 4. (The hook shown is a Gamakatsu F14.)
THREAD: Orange 8/0, 6/0, or 3/0 (I prefer 3/0).
TAILS: Pheasant-tail fibers.
CORE: Section cut from a foam cup.
ABDOMEN and THORAX: Dark orange-brown dubbing .
HACKLE: Dark brown or brown.
WING: Brown calf tail.
HEAD and COLLAR: Elk hair dyed dark brown.

Goldenrod

HOOK: Long shank, dry fly, size 8. (The hook shown is a Gamakatsu F-14.)
THREAD: Gold or yellow 8/0, 6/0, or 3/0 (I prefer 3/0).
TAILS: Pheasant-tail fibers.
CORE: Section cut from a foam cup.
ABDOMEN and THORAX: Gold dubbing.
HACKLE: Brown.
WING: Tan calf tail.
HEAD and COLLAR: Elk hair dyed gold (or substitute natural tan).

1. Start the thread at the bend. Dub the thread and build a small dubbing ball there. Tie in a bunch of three or four pheasant-tail fibers on each side of the ball—the result should be split tails.

2. Slide your fingers up the shank as you spiral the thread tightly up the pheasant butts and shank. Stop at three-quarters up the shank. Trim the butts.

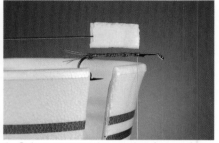

3. Snip a rectangular section from a foam cup as shown. The section should be long enough to reach from just ahead of the split tails to three quarters up the shank. The width of the section should allow it to wrap completely around the shank.

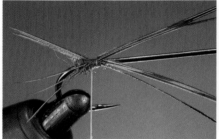

4. Wrap the section around the shank. Secure it with plenty of tight thread-turns. The thread-turns will compress the foam, so use the tightness of the turns and their placement to shape it. The foam should taper at its very ends and should be reduced somewhat throughout—remember that leaving the foam overthick will make the fly's body overthick, but that too much compression will reduce buoyancy. Actually, this is easy enough to judge. If you are in doubt, check these photographs.

5. Dub halfway up the shank, and then tie in a hackle. Trim the hackle's stem.

6. Dub to the front of the foam and then palmer the hackle forward in three to five turns. Secure the hackle's tip with thread, and then trim the tip.

7. Trim out the hackle fibers atop the thorax leaving a "V." Cut, comb, and stack a bunch of calf-tail fibers. Tie in the fibers as a wing that extends to the edge of the hook's bend or slightly beyond. Trim the fiber butts and cover them with tight thread-turns.

8. Advance the thread to just behind the eye. Snip, comb, and stack a bunch of elk hair. Hold the hair along the hook with the hairs' tips at the bend. Trim the hairs' butts to a straight edge at the eye's tip.

9. Work the cut ends of the butts down around the shank at the eye, tips projecting off the eye. Take two light thread-turns around the butts, and then pull the thread tight. Trim the butts and bind them with thread.

10. Wind the thread to just ahead of the body. Stroke back the hair and secure it with a tight thread-collar. This creates a bullet head. The thread should be tight enough to cause the hair tips to flair. Whip finish the thread around the collar and trim the thread.

11. Turn the Salmonrod upside down and trim away hackles and hair tips from its underside. Add cement to the thread collar to complete the Salmonrod.

12. Rod's newest, still-experimental version of the Salmonrod features rubber-strand legs. To tie it, omit the hackle. When wrapping the thread collar, loop a fine-diametered section of rubber-strand over the thread and then slide that strand down to one side of the bullet head. Add a few tight thread-turns and then add another section of rubber-strand on the other side of the bullet head. Whip finish the thread, trim it, trim the underside collar hairs, add cement to the thread collar. The strands should be dark-brown or black.

13. Trim the rubber-strand legs to length to complete this version of the Salmonrod. Here it is, completed. Note that this hair collar is short. A short collar is an option for both the standard and rubber-leg versions of both the Salmonrod and Goldenrod. The short hairs do not compete with hackle or rubber-strands in suggesting legs.

The Morrisfoam Diver

Foam in a floating bass fly makes a world of sense. Beyond the obvious value of its buoyancy, foam's supple resistance to a bass's bite suggests life–though a bass usually lets go of a hard balsa-popper after a touch, it may hang on to a soft-foam fly for several seconds. Several seconds means a very good chance of a hookup. Bass hang onto spun-hair flies too, but the Morrisfoam Diver is quicker to tie and floats longer.

My problem was that foam's extreme buoyancy resists diving–this is not good in a fly called a diver. Sometimes my divers *would* dive, but often as not they would just begin to bury their nose, and then pop back up and skip lightly. The hydrodynamics so carefully designed into their shape made little impression on them. That's the purpose of the lead–to help the foam submerge, to keep some noses buried–and it does a fine job. Generally, I'm easy going, but foam is one area in which I demand obedience. I tried other approaches, but as usual, the simplest proved best.

The Morrisfoam Diver was originally designed for large-mouth bass, and for them it has proven deadly. In smaller sizes it has turned out to be just as deadly for bluegills. One day on Barnes Butte Lake, a fee lake in central Oregon, my friends and I caught bass, enormous bluegills, and big rainbow and brown trout on a small, yellow Morristone Diver. It was great fun, but spooky. I felt as though we were somehow defying the gods of fly fishing. So I can't recommend the Morrisfoam Diver for rainbow and brown trout because I tried that once and got that same spooky feeling.

I want to try smallmouth bass on the Morrisfoam Diver, but I haven't found them willing to feed at the surface when I had Divers handy.

There is no reason to limit the Morrisfoam Diver to the colors shown, and the tail can be constructed of almost anything that soaks up lots of water–marabou, hackles, hair–anything that helps keep the Morristone Diver from traveling much after a chug, dive, or twitch. Bass cover is often so tight that a traveling bug is soon outside useful range. Feel free to experiment with the size of the foam collar, the length and thickness of the body, and the amount and placement of lead; changes in these will affect the performance of the finished Morrisfoam Diver–make it chug louder or lower or more sharply, make it dive more quickly or more gradually, make it dive deeper or shallower. Hook style will also affect performance. I am adding the optional rubber-strand legs more and more often. I can't prove that bass prefer rubber-strand legs, but apparently I do. When you are satisfied with a combination of all these variables, it may be worthwhile to take some notes. But all this aside, if you follow the instructions and photographs to come, you will end up with a fly that performs well.

Fish the Morrisfoam Diver around lily pads, logs and other shoreline cover. Sometimes a vigorous retrieve is best, but I usually fish it with dives, chugs, and twitches broken up by long pauses.

Morrisfoam Diver

HOOK: Heavy wire, short shank (bass–bug hook), sizes 6 to
2/0; for panfish, sizes 12 to 6. (The hook shown is a
Partridge CS41.)
THREAD: 3/0 (size–A rod–winding thread for big hooks) in a
color to match the foam.
WEIGHT: Lead wire.
TAIL: Triangle (or strip) of rabbit fur on the hide.
BODY and COLLAR: soft–foam.

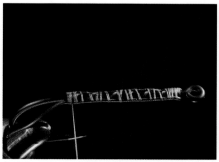

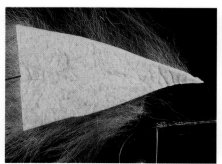

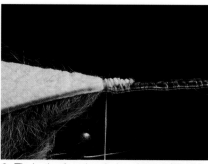

1. Mix up some slow-cure epoxy glue. Start the thread behind the eye. Secure a two-and-a-half-shank-long section of lead wire to the far side of the shank, just behind the eye; the wire should extend back to the bend. Bend the lead tightly around, under the eye. Secure the lead along the shank's near side just behind the eye, not obstructing the eye. Grasp the lead wire and slide your grasp down the lead and shank, holding the lead in place along the sides, as you secure the lead with tight spiraled thread-turns ending at the bend. Trim the lead at the bend. Add epoxy modestly all along the lead.

2. From a rabbit hide, cut a triangle that is long on two sides and shorter at the base; the fur should cant down from the tip of the triangle towards its base. It is best to cut the hide on its skin side with a razor blade, and don't cut too deeply or you'll shear off the tips of the fur along the strip's edges. The triangle should be about two hook-shanks in length.

3. Tie in the fur triangle by about 1/8" of its tip, fur down. (You can substitute a precut fur strip made for a fly called a Zonker, and that will work fine, but I prefer the triangle shape.)

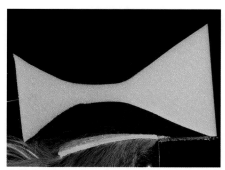

4. Cut a shape from foam as shown—a small triangular shape at one end, a straight stretch, then a larger triangle. The straight section should be about shank length.

(If you must use two layers of foam to obtain proper thickness, cut two shapes, one of proper size and another that is the same length but about 1/16" slimmer along each side; then tie in the larger foam pattern first and the slimmer one over it—the difference in pattern-size helps round out the finished foam body.)

Cutting Pattern for the Morrisfoam Diver

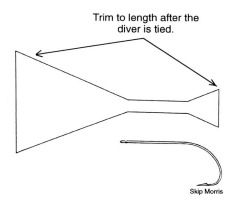

Trim to length after the diver is tied.

Skip Morris

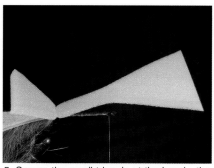

5. Secure the small triangle at the bend—the triangle should project up and back over the fur strip's tie-in point. Lift the foam that is over the shank and spiral the thread to the eye.

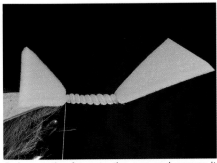

6. Lower the foam to the eye and secure it there with firm thread-turns. Spiral the thread down the shank and foam to the bend; use enough firm turns to compress the foam.

7. Fold the free foam back and down (stretching it slightly). Secure the foam's large triangle at the bend. Now there should be a tapered bulge of foam from the eye to the bend and a fan of foam over the fur strip. Add a Skip's whip (see section II, "Tying With Foam"), and then trim the thread. You can also add a generous dollop of epoxy to the Skip's whip *underneath*; this will further help the body resist shifting on the hook.

8. Trim the foam fan to a half-circle projecting about one shank's length beyond the bend.

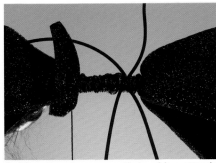

9. After step six, you can tie in rubber-strands for legs if you wish. Loop a strand over the thread, slide the strand to the shank, tighten the thread. Add another strand on the other side. Trim the strands later; trim them long. You may later have to trim the foam body around the legs to keep them from tipping too far down.

Notice that *two* foam shapes are used here on a particularly big hook.

The Morrisfoam Predator

Randall Kaufmann had a good idea: Add buoyancy to a dragonfly-nymph imitation and fish that imitation on a sinking line. Then the line will find bottom while the nymph hovers safely above lake-bed snags. This keeps the nymph down with fish but slightly above anything else it might hook.

Randall buoyed his nymph with spun deer hair, a reasonable solution. But this struck me as an ideal use for foam—deer hair eventually becomes waterlogged, especially when submerged, but foam remains buoyant almost indefinitely. Having since landed a lot of trout on Morrisfoam Predators, with few snag-ups between strikes, I am convinced that this use of foam *is* ideal.

The Morrisfoam Predator might not be the easiest foam fly to tie, but it's easy enough. I tie it in brown or olive, usually dark, but sometimes lighter. But you can tie the Morrisfoam Predator in whatever hue suggests the natural you are imitating. Dragonfly nymphs vary in color considerably. If I had to chose one all-purpose color for the

Morrisfoam Predator, it would be dark olive-brown, but I can't get that in precolored foam; my second choice would be dark brown. The legs can be medium or fine rubberstrand. The medium does a fine job, but the fine really jiggles to the twitch and I prefer it. Round rubber-strand still comes in few colors, hence the "dark" in the pattern. If I could, I'd use dark-brown strands for the brown version and dark-olive for the olive.

The word "Predator" in the name comes from the dragonfly nymph's aggressive feeding habits. Fish the Morrisfoam Predator in lakes and slow-moving streams, around weed beds, in the shallows, and well down. It can be worked slowly, with quick darts, or in combinations of both. Because this is a buoyant fly, the slower you retrieve it, the more angle you will have in your leader—the line is down, the fly is up. So if you retrieve the Morrisfoam Predator slowly, be prepared to set the hook immediately at the slightest suggestion of a take.

Morrisfoam Predator, Brown

HOOK: Heavy wire, 2X to 4X long, sizes 12 to 6. (The hook shown is an Orvis 1526.)
THREAD: Brown 3/0.
TAIL: Pheasant-tail fibers, short.
ABDOMEN: A strip of 1/8" thick dark-brown soft-foam.
HEAD and WING CASE: A strip of 1/16" dark-brown soft-foam.
EYES: Melted monofilament or preformed plastic dumbbell eyes.
LEGS: Dark rubber-strand.

Morrisfoam Predator, Olive

HOOK: Heavy wire, 2X to 4X long, sizes 12 to 6. (The hook shown is an Orvis 1526.)
THREAD: Olive or green 3/0.
TAIL: Pheasant-tail fibers, short.
ABDOMEN: A strip of 1/8" dark-olive soft-foam.
HEAD and WING CASE: A strip of 1/16" dark-olive soft-foam.
EYES: Melted monofilament or preformed plastic dumbbell eyes.
LEGS: Dark rubber-strand.

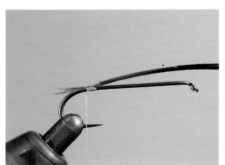

1. Start the thread at the bend; there, tie in about six pheasant-tail fibers, short. Trim the fibers' butts.

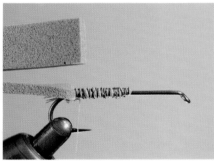

2. Cut a strip of 1/8" thick foam; its width should be slightly less than half the shank's length. Add a bit of slow-cure epoxy to the shank, and tie in the foam strip at the bend. Secure the foam along half the shank, and then trim the foam's end.

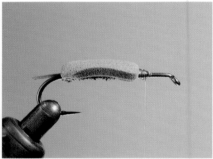

3. Advance the thread to a point three quarters up the shank; add some epoxy there. Pull the foam up and forward under moderate tension (stretch the foam slightly), secure it with thread-turns, trim the foam.

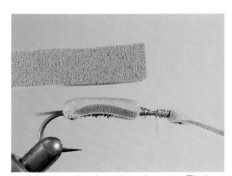

4. Advance the thread to the eye. Tie in a strip of 1/16" foam, about one-gape wide, right behind and projecting off the eye. (The 1/8" foam will work; it just looks a bit clumsy.) Trim the foam.

5. Just behind the hook's eye, tie in some plastic dumbbell eyes (melt your own from monofilament or buy them preformed) with crisscrossed thread-turns atop the shank.

6. Spiral the thread back to the front of the abdomen. Slip a looped section of rubber-strand down the thread to the shank and secure it on one side. Repeat this on the other side.

7. Draw back the rubber-strands and advance the thread to the rear of the plastic eyes. Pull the front end of one strand forward alongside the shank and secure it at the eyes with thread-turns. Do the same on the other side.

8. Spiral the thread back slightly (about 1/16") and then pull the front foam-strip up and back with a bit of stretch. Secure the strip there with thread-turns, add a Skip's whip (see section II, "Tying With Foam") over these turns, trim the thread.

9. Trim the the foam straight across, about one-third down the abdomen, and then cut a notch in its end.

10. Trim the legs to a length that gives a spider look. With marking pens, you can add to the Morrisfoam Predator's realism, but I'm usually in too much of a hurry to bother.

Brian Rose Photo

The Morrisfoam Dun and Bunse Dun

For my own Morrisfoam Dun I take no bows—it grew from Richard Bunse's concept. Richard deserves the real credit.

The Bunse Dun proves what I always suspected but couldn't prove through my own efforts—that a tough, buoyant adult-mayfly imitation with a natural upturned abdomen could be made from foam. My own attempts at a foam mayfly were off track until Richard's fly lit the way. Actually, it goes beyond a foam mayfly—*many* of my efforts at tying with foam bottomed out until Richard.

But the Bunse Dun is more than just a pathway to the real thing—it *is* the real thing. Yes, it takes a while to tie, but it's durable and buoyant and trout take it with confidence. Richard prefers Ethafoam for his dun; he feels that its transluscence mimics that of the natural.

The Bunse Green Drake Dun imitates its namesake—a large western mayfly called the green drake that hatches early in the season from quick water. There are several variations of the Bunse Dun, each an imitation of a specific mayfly species. The patterns for these variations are listed in section IV, "Additional Foam Flies."

My Morrisfoam Dun has a poly-yarn wing and parachute hackle and tying it is fairly quick—my own preferences worked out of Richard's fly. The bright-yellow wing can be traded for a more subtle, more natural color, but I like the yellow for three reasons: I believe that wings are the component least noticed by trout in a floating insect or fly; I believe that fly wings tend to lose their color against a light sky (hold a yellow-wing fly skyward, as a trout would see it, and see for yourself; and in the scant light of a dark sky, wing color won't matter at all); and I find yellow wings much easier for me to see than any other color, especially if I'm wearing polarized dark glasses. Of course you can use colors in the wing of the Morrisfoam Dun that precisely imitate specific mayflies if you wish. A significant difference between my dun and Richard's is that I use soft-foam rather than Ethafoam (though Richard's transluscence argument *is* convincing).

You will have to choose between the Morrisfoam Dun and Bunse Dun based on your preferences. Of course you may find that you prefer one or the other for specific conditions. Or you could tie up plenty of both and fish whichever strikes your fancy at the moment. Neither Richard nor I will mind.

Morrisfoam Dun Dark

HOOK: Short shank, dry fly, sizes 20 to 8. (The hook shown is a Dai-Riki 305.)
THREAD: Brown 8/0 or 6/0.
WING: Bright-yellow poly yarn.
HACKLE: One, brown.
BODY: Brown soft-foam. Because Morrisfoam Duns use denser foam than Bunse Duns, they also use thinner foam sheeting than do Bunse Duns–about 1/32" for the smallest hooks, up to about 1/16" for the largest.

Morrisfoam Dun Light

HOOK: Short shank, dry fly, sizes 20 to 8. (The hook shown is a Dai-Riki 305.)
THREAD: Tan 8/0 or 6/0.
WING: Bright-yellow poly yarn.
HACKLE: One, ginger.
BODY: Tan soft-foam. (The foam shown is actually peach, because currently I can't get precolored tan. Any color that is light and subtle is fine. See the pattern for the Morrisfoam Dun Dark, above, for foam thicknesses.)

NOTE: Like the Bunse Dun, the Morrisfoam Dun can be tied in a wide range of sizes and colors to imitate specific mayflies.

1. Start the thread just ahead of midshank. There, tie in a length of poly yarn atop the hook with tight crisscrossed thread-turns. This will set the yarn at a right angle to the shank.

2. Draw up the tips of the yarn and take a tight turn of thread around its base (instructions for poly-yarn parachute-hackle wings usually rotate the poly under the hook before drawing up the wing, but not here). Wrap thread up the yarn's base about 1/16" and then back down to the hook; use light to moderate thread-tension so that you needn't hold the wing.

3. Strip the base of a hackle that gauges one size larger than the hook's size. Hold the hackle alongside the thread-turns at the yarn's base, and then wrap another layer of thread up and then down the yarn. This secures the hackle. You can use plenty of thread tension this time. Draw the hackle's stem back along the shank, secure it with thread-turns, trim the stem.

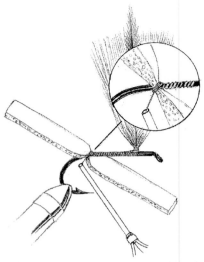

4. Wrap the thread to the bend and half hitch it there. (You can add a tiny bit of epoxy here to toughen the fly if you like.) Cut a gape-wide strip of foam (this will produce a plump high-floating fly; cut a slimmer strip for a more exact imitation). Remove the hook from your vise. Push the point of the hook through the foam, a shank's length from the foam's end, in the center of the foam strip. Return the hook to your vise.

5. Secure the foam at the bend, with the shank's-length end of the foam atop the hook, projecting rearwards. Take two firm turns of thread that go over the hook *behind* the foam and under the hook *in front of* the foam—this will tip the rearward end of the foam up. (See the illustration.)

1. Secure the foam at the bend with a few snug thread-turns.

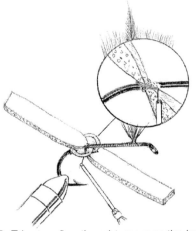

2. Take two firm thread turns *over* the hook *behind* the foam and *under* the hook in *front* of the foam.

6. Advance the thread to the hook's eye. Pull the front of the foam forward and up; stretch it slightly. Take a loose turn of thread over the foam and then pull that turn tight. The foam should swell up around the sides of the shank. Add three more thread-turns to really secure the foam.

7. Stretch the foam's stub-end tight, and trim it away. Trim the foam, where it projects off the bend, to a slender taper. (Or trim it later, when the fly is complete.)

8. Wind the hackle down the thread-turns at the wing's base. Use tight, close turns. Drape the tip of the hackle over the eye and let your hackle pliers hang. Add tight thread-turns to secure the hackle's tip.

9. Draw back the front hackle fibers and trim the hackle's tip. Build a thread head. Whip finish the thread, trim it, add head cement.

10. Trim the wing to a point. The wing's length is measured against the foam body; the wing should equal the full length of the foam body or slightly shorter. For increased hook-point clearance, take out a snip of foam from the underside of the thorax. This weakens the foam, but thus far it's caused me no problems.

11. Here is how to tie a variation on the Morrisfoam Dun which I call the Skip's Sequel. Cut, comb, stack, measure, and tie in a bunch of deer hair at midshank (instructions for this are described in detail for the next fly, the Bunse Dun). Wind the thread to the bend and half hitch it there. Cut a strip of soft-foam and push the hook's point through it, and then secure the foam and tip its end up with thread-turns (as described for the Morrisfoam Dun).

12. Press your thumb nail down against the shank and up and back against the hair. The purpose is to crease the hair upright into a fan shape. Repeat the thumb-nail technique, if needed, to get all the hair up. You can press from the sides too.

13. Pull the hair back and secure it upright with tight thread-turns against its front. Use plenty of turns. If you gently draw the foam back out of your way as you draw back the hair, it will make this step easier.

14. Advance the thread to the eye. Pull the foam strip forward and up under the shank. Secure it there with a few thread-turns. Stretch the end of the foam a bit and trim it closely. The tightness and width of the foam strip will determine how the hair lies at the sides; I prefer the hair to project straight out at the sides, a half circle of hair over the top of the shank, more or less.

15. Whip finish the thread, trim it, add head cement to the whip finish, taper the abdomen (as described for the Morrisfoam Dun). Here is the completed Skip's Sequel.

Bunse Green Drake Dun

HOOK: Short shank, dry fly, size 12. (The hook shown is a Mustad 94838.)
THREAD: Yellow 6/0 or 8/0.
BODY: Ethafoam sheeting colored green (see section II, "Tying With Foam"). For all Bunse Dun patterns: use foam 3/64" thick for hook sizes 20 and 18; 1/16" for hook sizes 16 and 14; 3/32" for size 12 and larger.
TAILS: Two mink–tail, nutria, or beaver guard hairs.
WING: Natural dun–colored coastal deer hair.

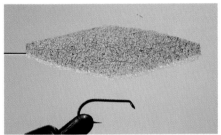

1 Color a section of Ethafoam sheeting and secure the color as described in section II, "Tying With Foam." (Or color the foam and then wait to brush on the thinned Flexament *after* the fly is complete; I prefer this because it secures all the thread-turns.) Cut the colored foam into a diamond shape approximately three full hook-lengths long by one hook-length wide. Color the edges of the diamond if you like.

2. Mount a beading needle by its eye in your vise as shown. Start the thread lightly near the needle's center. Tie in one tip of the foam diamond on the far side of the needle. The uncolored flat of the foam should face you and the bulk of the diamond should project away from the vise. Use light thread-tension throughout the needle-tying.

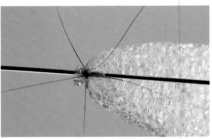

3. A tiny hump of foam should project beyond the thread-turns. Hold one tail hair above the foam and one below, take a light turn of thread around both, pull the turn snug enough to spread the tails. The tails should project about two shank-lengths from their tie-in point, but this is not critical. Do not trim the tails' butts.

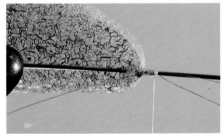

4. Bend back the diamond as shown, towards the vise. Wind the thread down the needle and hair butts a turn or two.

5. Bring the foam forward again, and then take two thread-turns over it. The turns should be just tight enough to form a round foam-segment.

6. Continue forming segments, each slightly larger than the last, until there are four. (The hump of foam between the tails counts as a segment.) Half hitch the thread and trim it. Slide the segmented abdomen off the needle.

7. Remove the needle from your vise. Mount a hook in your vise. Start the thread halfway up the shank; at this point tie in some combed, stacked coastal deer hair. The hair should project one-and-a-half hook shanks from its tie-in point. Trim the butts of the hair at an angle, and then bind the butts with tight thread-turns. End with the thread at the bend. Half hitch the thread but don't cut it.

8. Remove the hook from your vise. Push the hook's point through the center and out the bottom of the last segment of the foam, opposite the seam. Slide the foam up to the bend. Return the hook to your vise. Take two turns of thread around the half-hitched thread that forms the last foam segment.

9. Draw the foam down out of the way; then spiral the thread tightly to just behind the eye, catching up the tail butts as you go. Trim the butts closely. With your thumb nail, crease the hair back and up, and then add tight thread-turns at the front of the hair to secure it upright.

10. Advance the thread to the eye again. With your left hand (right handers), draw the front of the foam up against and around the sides of the shank. Add firm thread-turns at the eye to secure the foam there.

11. Stretch the end of the foam as you trim it closely.

Spiral the thread back between the eye and the wing and take a full turn there. Then spiral the thread *beneath* the wing to about halfway between the wing and bend. Take two turns there, spiral the thread *forward* under the wing, and then take a turn between the wing and the eye. Return the thread to the eye, build a thread head, add a whip finish, trim the thread. (See the illustrations for thread wrapping the thorax.) Remember that, as Richard describes it, the tightness and placement of the thread-turns "sculpts" the thorax.

12. Cut a tiny slit in the foam on each side of the wing. Don't cut the thread! (You have the option of cutting the slits before thread wrapping the thorax—Richard prefers this—but for at least your first few Bunse Duns, I'd suggest cutting them after.)

Thread Wrapping Thorax

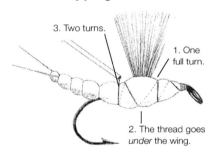

3. Two turns.

1. One full turn.

2. The thread goes *under* the wing.

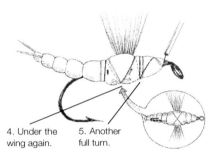

4. Under the wing again.

5. Another full turn.

13. Pull the wing's hairs to the sides, into the slits. The wing should now form a fan, a half-circle.

14. If needed, trim down the stub of foam between the tails, and touch up the foam wherever needed with a marking pen. Add a drop of highly thinned Flexament (three parts thinner to one part Flexament) to the tail, to both of the wing slits, and to the thread head (I don't bother with head cement). If you haven't yet secured the foam's color, simply add Flexament at the points just described and wherever needed to coat the color. Remember, thinned Flexament flows well—a little is a lot.

The Morrisfoam Stones

Those-in-the-know will tell you that to the trout fisher, the golden stone is just as important as the famous salmonfly, perhaps even *more* important. That is, they will tell you this if they are first given sodium pentothal. That's the problem with those-in-the-know: They like to know what those-not-in-the-know *don't* know. But I know what they know, which is why I can now tell you what those-in-the-know, know. And it's time you knew.

Each spring or early summer (here in Oregon it's around mid-May; in the Rocky Mountains it's about a month later), giant, corpulent orange-bellied stoneflies called salmonflies begin emerging from and fluttering about a few western rivers. Regardless of what trout do, anglers go into a frenzy, generally a sort of quiet frenzy, but it still counts as frenzy. Around Portland, Oregon, fly fishers all seem to be planning trips and with raised eyebrows saying, "I hear the salmonflies are coming off the Deschutes" and asking, "What have you heard about the salmonflies?" I like seeing fly fishers excited–it's got to be good for our sport, overall. But they never get this excited over the golden stone, and that seems a little crazy.

The golden stonefly hatches from nearly every western river that has some quick water, in other words nearly every western river. But the salmonfly emerges in significant numbers from only a precious few rivers. Therefore, the golden-stone hatch is the more common and more accessible of the two. In the Deschutes River, the salmonfly shows first, followed soon by the golden. Their hatches often overlap. In my experience, the goldens come off the Deschutes in roughly equal numbers to the salmonflies. So here is a great salmonfly river, and yet it produces just as many golden stones.

My friends-in-the-know (don't worry, I won't start into *that* again)–who include guides, outdoor writers, and even an entomologist–agree that the golden's habit of dropping to the water to release its eggs makes it more available to trout than the salmonfly, which usually performs an aerial egg release.

The points behind all of this are (1) that the golden stone-fly is of vital importance to the western fly fisher and (2) that I'm going to show you how to tie my soft-foam imitation of one. Though I'll tie my golden-stone version, the tying of the salmonfly version is identical. The only differences between the two flies are color and, sometimes, size.

No easier or harder to tie than the Bunse Dun, the Morrisfoam Golden Stone and Morrisfoam Salmonfly have proved themselves on western trout. I invite you to prove them on eastern trout. (After all, they could easily be adapted for imitating eastern stones.)

In a stonefly imitation, foam and an extended body are a blessing–they help keep the fly afloat in swift, broken currents. Stoneflies hatch from such water, so the adults often wind up back in it. But often enough, stonefly adults wind up in gentle back eddies and quiet water where trout have plenty of opportunity for close inspection. For their clean outline and detail, the Morrisfoam stones fish here as well as they do in fast water.

My greatest experience is with Morrisfoam stones of Ethafoam, but I like what soft-foam has to offer–greater durability, inherent color–so I now use it more often.

Morrisfoam Golden Stone

HOOK: Short shank (regular shank as an alternate), dry fly, size 8. (The hook shown is a Tiemco 921.)
THREAD: Gold or yellow 3/0.
TAILS: A tan (or brown) turkey flat (or other body feather).
BODY: Antique–gold soft–foam (or a similar color such as yellow or yellow colored over with a gold marking pen–I don't think exact color is critical) or colored Ethafoam, about 1/8″ to 3/16″ thick.
WING: Ethafoam colored tan (or brown), 1/16″ thick or less.
LEGS: Tan (or brown, yellow, or gold) medium– or fine–diameter round rubber–strands.
HEAD and BACK: The same foam used for the body.

Morrisfoam Salmonfly

HOOK: Short shank (regular shank as an alternate), dry fly, sizes 8 and 6. (The hook shown is a Tiemco 921.)
THREAD: Orange 3/0.
TAILS: Brown (or black) turkey flat (or other body feather).
BODY: Orange soft–foam marked with a dark–brown marking pen until the orange is subdued or Ethafoam, about 1/8″ to 1/4″ thick.
WING: Ethafoam colored brown, about 1/16″ thick or less.
LEGS: Brown (or black) medium– or fine–diameter round rubber–strands.
HEAD and BACK: The same foam used for the body.

1. Mount a beading needle in your vise. Lightly start the thread on the needle. Strip the fibers from the sides of the tail feather; then snip the center from the tip leaving short split-tails.

2. Mix up some epoxy and dab a tiny amount onto the thread-turns. Tie in the tail feather by its stem as shown.

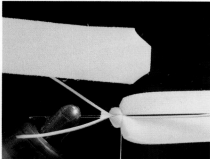

3. Snip a strip of foam about one-shank wide. Trim the edges at one end of the strip to a short, blunt taper as shown. Tie in the tip of the taper at the feather's tie-in point, on the far side of the needle.

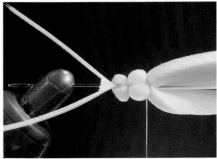

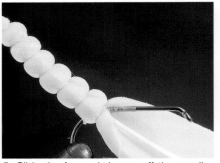

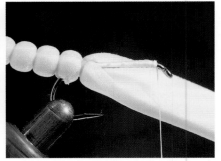

4. Advance the thread a turn or two over both the needle and the stem (not the foam); then form a segment in the foam with two snug thread-turns. Continue forming segments in this manner until there are six or seven. (See "The Morrisfoam Dun and Bunse Dun" under the Bunse Dun for more instruction on forming foam segments.) Add a Skip's whip over the last thread-turns (see section II, "Tying With Foam"), and then trim the thread.

5. Slide the foam abdomen off the needle. Remove the needle from your vise. Mount a hook in your vise. Start the thread at about midshank, spiral it to the bend, half hitch it there, remove the hook from your vise. Push the hook's point through the center and out the bottom of the last segment, opposite the seam. Return the hook to your vise.

6. Add a bit of epoxy at the hook's bend, secure the last foam segment with a few new thread-turns over the old, spiral the thread over both shank and feather stem to the eye. Trim the stem.

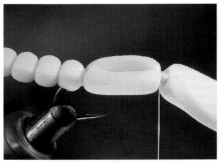

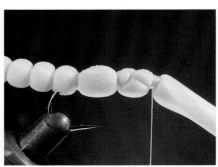

Thread Wrapping The Thorax

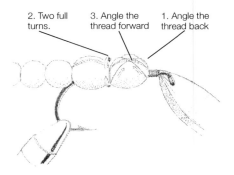

2. Two full turns.   3. Angle the thread forward   1. Angle the thread back

7. Add a bit of epoxy along the shank, up to the eye. Lift the foam up and forward, and then secure it at the eye with several thread-turns. Work the thread back in a few turns, 1/16" or slightly more; this should form a short thread collar.

8. Angle the thread back over the *top* of the abdomen to about midshank. Take two full turns there. Again over the top, angle the thread forward to the front of the foam abdomen. The abdomen now has two segments and the thread should cross itself over the front segment.

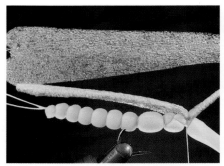

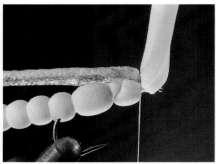

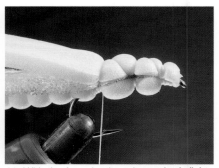

9. Cut a wing from thin foam-sheeting in the shape shown. (I still use colored Ethafoam for this.) Tie in the wing behind the eye, projecting back over the body. The wing should reach a bit beyond the end of the abdomen.

10. Trim the stub end of the wing's base. Work the thread to the rear of the thread collar behind the eye. Pull the front of the foam up, and then tightly back. The eye will push right through Ethafoam; but if you've used a soft-foam, you may have to poke a hole in it with your scissor tips for the eye to reach through.

11. With the foam back and stretched slightly, take a few tight securing thread-turns. Angle the thread back over the first segment, and then take one full turn of thread. Angle the thread back over the second segment, and then take a full turn there. The thread should now be at the bend.

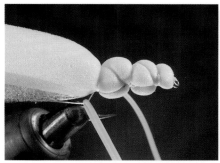

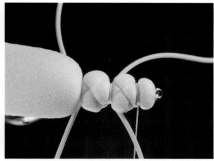

12. Loop a short section of rubber-strand over the thread and slide the section to one side of the hook. Do the same on the other side. Draw the strands back out of your way and angle the thread forward over the foam segment. Take a full turn of thread at the front of that segment.

13. Pull one, then the other, rubber-strand forward and secure both to the sides of the abdomen.

14. Draw the strands back out of your way again, and then advance the thread forward over the next segment—this should leave the thread at the thread-turns just behind the head. Add a Skip's whip, and then trim the thread.

Thread Wrapping The Head And Back

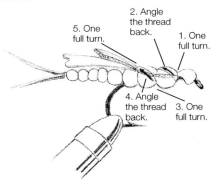

5. One full turn.

2. Angle the thread back.

1. One full turn.

4. Angle the thread back.

3. One full turn.

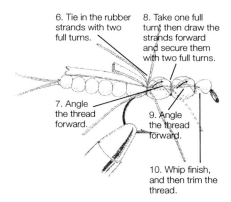

6. Tie in the rubber strands with two full turns.

8. Take one full turn, then draw the strands forward and secure them with two full turns.

7. Angle the thread forward.

9. Angle the thread forward.

10. Whip finish, and then trim the thread.

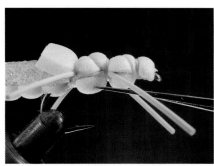

15. If it is too long, trim the end of the foam where it extends over the wing. Trim the legs to stonefly-length. If there is a bulge of foam obstructing the eye from beneath, trim it away and trim the underside of the thorax if the gape seems crowded. Color the body with a marking pen if needed. The Morrisfoam Stone is complete—just try to sink it.

Trimming Under The Eye

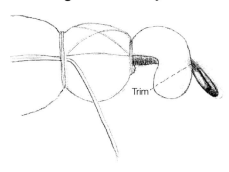

Trim

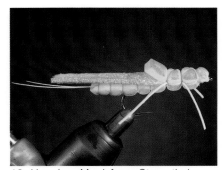

16. Here is a Morrisfoam Stone tied on a long-shank hook. Simply create three or four segments on the needle, the rest on the shank. Sometimes a regular or long-shank hook can balance this fly, and hook fish that are nipping at the fly rather than taking it whole.

ADDITIONAL FOAM FLIES

Balloon Caddis
Roman Moser

HOOK: Partridge Roman Moser Arrow Point (light wire, 1X short), size 12.
THREAD: Yellow 8/0 or 6/0.
ABDOMEN: Olive synthetic dubbing.
WING: Natural or dyed deer hair.
HEAD and THORAX: Golden-yellow soft-foam.

COMMENTS: The foam suggests a bursting shuck.

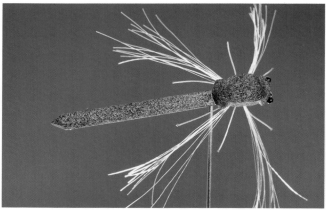

Betts' Foam Dragonfly
John Betts

HOOK: Short shank, medium to light wire (sizes aren't given, but the hook in the sample fly John gave me looks to be size 6).
THREAD: Green 3/0.
LEGS: 50-pound dacron colored green and blue with a marking pen or green and blue rubber-strands. Six legs.
WINGS: Clear nylon jig hair, divided into four wings.
ABDOMEN: A Strip of 1/4" thick white Evasote cut into a long stip with a point on the end. Color the strip chartreuse on the sides and bottom, blue on top.
BACK and HEAD: A 3/8" thick strip of white soft-foam colored as the abdomen is.
THORAX: Chartreuse Furry Foam.
EYES: Steel dressmaker's pins with black heads.

Betts' Red Flying Ant
John Betts

HOOK: Standard dry fly, ring eye, sizes 18 to 12.
THREAD: White 8/0 or 6/0.
ABDOMEN and HEAD: White Evasote colored with a red marking pen.
WINGS: Zing Wing cut to shape.
HACKLE: Brown, a few turns just behind the foam head. Trim the fibers closely underneath.

COMMENTS: The foam is tied in slightly down the bend, secured just short of midshank, compressed fine by thread-turns to the eye; then the front of the foam is doubled back and secured. Next come wings and hackle. I've seen trout in Pacific Northwest lakes feed heavily on reddish flying ants.

Black Legged Waterwalker
Bruce E. James

HOOK: Light wire, 2X long, sizes 10 to 6.
THREAD: Black 6/0; black 3/0 for the head.
BODY: A wrapped layer of black or gray soft-foam coated with Flexament, then wrapped lightly with black dubbing.
WING: White calf tail (optional).
BULLET HEAD and COLLAR: Natural elk hair.
LEGS: Black rubber-strands.

Bunse Hex Dun
Richard Bunse

HOOK: Short shank, dry fly, sizes 8 to 6.
THREAD: Yellow 8/0, 6/0 or 3/0.
BODY: Ethafoam sheeting colored yellow. (See section II, "Tying With Foam" and "The Morrisfoam Dun and Bunse Dun.")
TAILS: Two mink–tail, nutria, or beaver guard hairs. (I use Micro Fibetts.)
WING: Bleached coastal deer hair (I sometimes use regular deer or soft elk).

Bunse Pale Morning Dun
Richard Bunse

HOOK: Short shank, dry fly, size 18.
THREAD: Yellow 8/0 or 6/0.
BODY: Ethafoam sheeting colored pale yellow. (See section II, "Tying With Foam" and "The Morrisfoam Dun and Bunse Dun.")
TAILS: Two mink–tail, nutria, or beaver guard hairs.
WING: Bleached coastal deer hair.

Bunse Little Olive Dun
Richard Bunse

HOOK: Short shank, dry fly, sizes 20 to 18.
THREAD: Olive 8/0 or 6/0.
BODY: Ethafoam sheeting colored olive. (See section II, "Tying With Foam" and "The Morrisfoam Dun and Bunse Dun.")
TAILS: Two mink–tail, nutria, or beaver guard hairs.
WING: Natural dun–colored coastal deer hair.

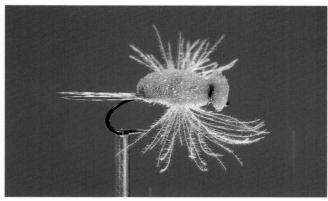

CDC Emerging Midge
Rene' Harrop

HOOK: 3X light, regular shank, sizes 20 to 14.
THREAD: Olive 8/0 or 6/0.
TAIL: Teal–flank fibers.
LEGS: Gray CDC.
BACK: Gray soft–foam.
BODY: Olive poly dubbing.
HEAD: Trimmed foam–butt from the back.

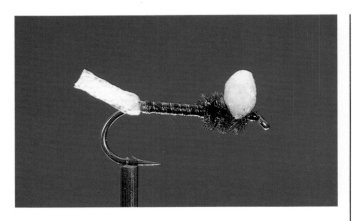

Chironomid Suspender Pupa

Doug Jorgensen

HOOK: Standard dry fly, sizes 20 to 12.
THREAD: Black 8/0 or 6/0.
PONTOON and TAIL: A Single Ethafoam strip, doubled for the pontoon.
RIB: Fine gold wire.
ABDOMEN: A slim Ethafoam strip, colored black with a marking pen.
THORAX: Peacock herl.

Ensolite Hopper

Richard Bunse

HOOK: Long shank, dry fly, sizes 12 to 8.
THREAD: Yellow or tan size–A Nymo.
RUMP: Tip of the Ensolite foam body.
BODY: White Ensolite cylinder (Richard shapes his own) colored yellow or green with a marking pen. The hook's point is pushed through the foam near the cylinder's end–this leaves a stub of foam off the bend and the front of the foam free. The foam is secured with thread–turns, the thread is advanced up the shank, the foam is secured again, and so on to create the segmented body.
LEGS: Knotted pheasant–tail fibers.
HEAD and COLLAR: Spun and shaped natural deer hair.

Creature

Gary LaFontain

HOOK: Steelhead dry fly, sizes 8 to 2.
THREAD: Black or brown 3/0.
BODY: Hard–foam secured with thread, then overwrapped with a brown or gray rabbit–hide fur strip, fur out.
TAIL: The tip of the fur strip used for the body, tapered and shaved.
HEAD: Rabbit fur cut from the body strip, dubbed.

COMMENTS: As Gary writes, this fly suggests "a mouse or some other animal swimming in the water."

Floating Snail

John Shewey

HOOK: Heavy wire, 2X long, sizes 14 to 8.
THREAD: Black 8/0 or 6/0.
WEIGHT: Only a few turns of lead wire at the bend.
FOOT: Black soft–foam.
BODY: Dark–olive or dark–gray chenille, built up to a taper.
HACKLE: One turn of partridge flank.

COMMENTS: Strange as it may seem, snails sometimes float at the surface of trout lakes in (and this is really stretching the term) hatches.

Foam Back Humpy
Phil Camera

HOOK: Standard dry fly, sizes 18 to 12.
THREAD: Yellow.
TAIL: Brown hackle fibers.
BODY: The working thread over the tail butts and foam butt.
HUMP: A Strip of soft-foam (tan or white, I think).
WINGS: Tan poly yarn. (In *Fly Tying With Synthetics*, where I found the Foam Back Humpy, the wings are described as "dubbing," but I think that "yarn" is correct.)
HACKLE: Brown.

COMMENTS: It was difficult to dig out some of the details on this one, but I doubt they are critical anyway.

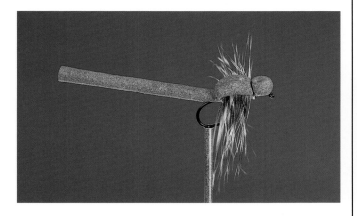

Foam Damsel

HOOK: Standard dry fly, sizes 14 and 12.
THREAD: Blue or black 8/0 or 6/0.
ABDOMEN, BACK and HEAD: Blue cylindrical soft-foam.
WINGS: Grizzly hackle palmered over the shank and trimmed top and bottom.

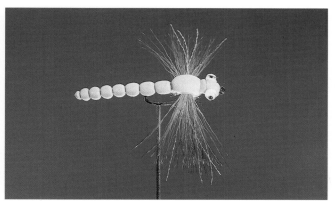

Foam Dragonfly
David Lucca

HOOK: Wide gape, straight eye. (A typical bass hook from what I can tell; no sizes given.)
THREAD: Blue 8/0, 6/0 or 3/0. (I prefer the 3/0.)
ABDOMEN: Gray soft-foam. (Tied on a needle, I assume, like the Bunse Dun.)
WINGS: Fine deer hair, spent.
THORAX: Gray dubbing.
HEAD and BACK: The foam butt from the abdomen.
EYES: Premade hollow plastic eyes, glued in place. (I consider these optional.)

COMMENTS: The segmented foam-body is secured at the rear of the shank, pulled *over* the thorax and wings and secured behind the hook eye. The thread is worked back, and then the foam is pulled up and back and secured to create the head. Trim the foam's free end, behind the head, and complete the Foam Dragonfly with the usual whip finish (or Skip's whip) and head cement. Largemouth bass sometimes feed heavily on dragonfly adults.

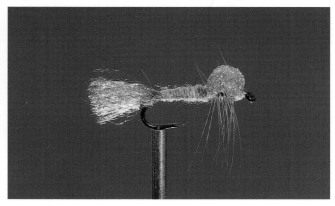

Foam Flav Emerger
Craig Mathews and John Juracek

HOOK: Standard dry fly, sizes 16 and 14.
THREAD: Olive 8/0 or 6/0.
SHUCK: Brown Z-lon.
ABDOMEN: Olive dubbing.
WING CASE: Gray Polycelon foam (or another soft-foam).
HACKLE: Grizzly or blue-dun hackle, trimmed beneath.

COMMENTS: "Flav" refers to *Drunella flavilinea*, a western evening-hatching mayfly.

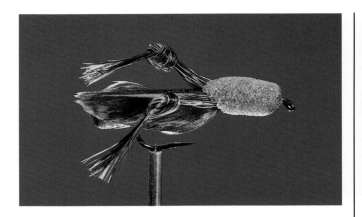

Foam Hopper
Dick Talleur

HOOK: Standard dry fly, size 10.
THREAD: Green 8/0 or 6/0.
BODY: Green soft-foam cylinder, melted at the rear end to rounded.
WING: Pheasant church window feather treated with Pliobond or Flexament.
LEGS: Fox squirrel hair, knotted. (From Dick Talleur's description in *The Versatile Fly Tyer*, I am not certain whether this is red-fox or gray-fox squirrel, but I prefer red.)
HEAD: A short section from a green soft-foam cylinder melted at the end to a round shape, same foam as for the body.

COMMENTS: Smash the barb. Wrap a layer of thread over the shank, whip finish the thread, cut its end. Push the foam body over the hook's point and three quarters up the shank; some foam should extend off the bend. Start the thread again up the shank and secure the foam. Add the pheasant feather, then the knotted legs; then trim the thread. Push a needle through the head, and then slip it over the eye and glue it in place.

Foam Midge Emerger
Craig Mathews and Verlyn Klinkenburg

HOOK: Standard dry fly, sizes 26 to 16.
THREAD: Gray 8/0 or 6/0.
SHUCK: Amber or olive Z-lon.
RIB: Fine copper wire.
ABDOMEN: Black, gray or yellow Polycelon foam (or another soft-foam).
LEGS: Partridge-flank feather fibers.
THORAX: Peacock herl.

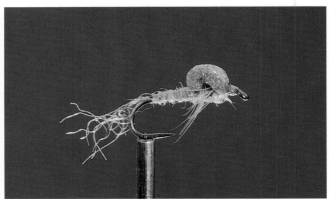

Foam Pale Morning Dun Emerger
Craig Mathews and John Juracek

HOOK: Standard dry fly, sizes 18 and 16.
THREAD: Yellow 8/0 or 6/0.
SHUCK: Brown Z-lon.
ABDOMEN: Orange-yellow beaver or rabbit fur in a dubbing loop.
WING CASE: Gray Polycelon foam (or another soft-foam).
HACKLE: Dun starling hackle.

COMMENTS: This imitates the pale-morning-dun mayfly.

Gray Foam Caddis
Dave Hughes

HOOK: Standard dry fly, sizes 18 to 10.
THREAD: Tan 8/0 or 6/0.
BODY: A strip of smokey-tan soft-foam. A gape-long rounded tab should extend over the bend; the remainder of the body is formed in two segments.
HACKLE: Light blue-dun, trimmed to a "V" below.
WING: Gray-dyed deer or elk hair.
HEAD: Trimmed wing butts.

Halo Emerger
Gary LaFontain

HOOK: Standard dry fly, sizes 24 to 8.
THREAD: 8/0 in a color to match the body.
TAG: Clear Antron wrapped partway down the bend and back.
TAIL: Marabou fibers in a color to match the body.
THORAX: A strip of white soft-foam tied atop and across the shank.
BODY: Fine poly dubbing in a color to match the natural. Dub around the foam thorax also.
WING: Elk or deer hair dyed orange. The butts are free, and trimmed close.

COMMENTS: The Halo Emerger suggests a mayfly nymph struggling at the surface to escape its shuck.

Kor–N–Popper
Keith Goltz

HOOK: Standard dry fly, sizes 16 to 8.
THREAD: Red 8/0, 6/0, or 3/0.
TAG: Yellow floss.
RIB: Red Krystal Flash.
BODY: White soft-foam strip (wound, I assume).
WING: White marabou.
THORAX: Yellow soft-foam.
COLLAR: Foam from the end of the wing case, short.

COMMENTS: According to *Fly Patterns of Alaska*, the Kor–N–Popper is actually a lake fly for trout–unusual trout fly.

Heathen
Phil Camera

HOOK: Light wire, short shank, humped shank, sizes 20 to 16.
THREAD: Black 8/0 or 6/0.
UNDERBODY: Pearl Krystal Flash.
OVERBODY: Gray Larva Lace (#08) slipped over the Krystal Lace-wrapped shank, secured at the rear with thread, and then ribbed forward with the thread.
WING: A post of white soft-foam.
THORAX: Hare's mask fur, dubbed heavily all around the foam post.

COMMENTS: This is an imitation of an emerging midge.

Madison River Stopper
Nick Nicklas

HOOK: Standard dry fly, sizes 14 to 10.
THREAD: Yellow 3/0.
BODY: Yellow soft-foam.
UNDERWING: Golden-pheasant tippet strands.
WING: Deer hair.
HEAD: Trimmed butts of the deer-hair wing.

COMMENTS: A simple fast-water imitation of the grasshopper or golden stonefly.

Mutant Ninja Cicada
Emmett Heath

HOOK: Long shank, dry fly, sizes 10 to 6.
THREAD: Orange 3/0.
BODY: Black soft-foam.
UNDERWING: Gold Krystal Flash.
OVERWING: Natural deer hair.
LEGS: Black or brown medium-diameter rubber-strand.
HACKLE: Grizzly, one or two.

Olive Foam Caddis
Dave Hughes

HOOK: Standard dry fly, sizes 18 to 10.
THREAD: Olive 8/0 or 6/0.
BODY: A strip of dark-green soft-foam. A rounded gape-long tab should project over the bend; the remainder of the body is formed in two segments.
HACKLE: Dark blue dun, trimmed to a "V" beneath.
WING: Natural-dun deer hair.
HEAD: Trimmed wing butts.

Natant Nymph
Charles Brooks

HOOK: 2X long, size 18 to 8. (The wire thickness isn't given, but I assume it's light wire.)
THREAD: Brown or tan 8/0 or 6/0.
PONTOON: Some kind of foam in a pouch made from nylon stockings.
TAIL: Grouse-flank or grizzly-hen fibers.
RIB: Fine gold wire.
BODY: Black, brown, gray, or tan wool yarn.
HACKLE: Beard of grouse-flank or grizzly-hen fibers.

Ovipositing Stone
Richard Bunse

HOOK: Standard dry fly, sizes 10 and 8.
THREAD: Gold, yelow or tan 8/0 or 6/0.
ABDOMEN: Segmented Ethafoam colored with a gold marking pen. (See instructions for the Bunse Dun in "The Morrisfoam Dun and Bunse Dun" section for creating the segmented body on a needle.)
WING: Natural deer or elk hair, extending to the rear of the abdomen.
HACKLE: Ginger and brown, heavy.

COMMENTS: The Ovipositing Stone imitates the golden stonefly and is meant to roll and skate with the wind.

PC Hopper
Phil Camera

HOOK: Standard dry fly, sizes 12 to 8.
THREAD: Dark 8/0 or 6/0.
OVERBODY: Yellow soft-foam strip.
UNDERBODY: Red ostrich herl.
UNDERWING: Deer hair.
LEGS: Brown hackle stems, stripped.
OVERWING: Imitation fern leaf folded and colored with a marking pen or a section of turkey primary glued to nylon stockings.
HACKLE: Brown.

COMMENTS: Start the thread at the eye, tie in the herl there, wind the thread to the bend, wind the ostrich to the bend and secure and trim it. Tie in the foam at the bend, spiral the thread forward a bit (through the herl), lower and secure the foam to create another segment. Create three segments and then tie the fly as usual.

Rainy's Stonefly
Rainy Riding

HOOK: Long shank, dry fly, sizes 10 to 2.
THREAD: Orange 8/0, 6/0, or 3/0.
TAIL: Natural light elk hair.
BODY: Orange Rainy's Float Foam.
RIB: Dark furnace hackle, trimmed.
UNDERWING: Pearl Krystal Flash.
WING: Natural light elk hair.
HACKLE: Brown, heavy.

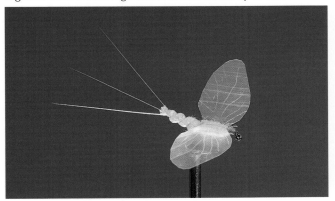

Poly–Foam Spinner
Bill Blackstone

HOOK: Short shank, dry fly (probably size 22 to 12).
THREAD: Light-yellow 8/0.
TAILS: Three bristles from a Simmons White Sable paint brush or three Micro Fibetts.
ABDOMEN: A strip of poly 2D foam trimmed to a point. The abdomen is tied on a needle and then slid free when complete. (I don't know what poly 2D foam is, but Bill says that electronics stores have scads of it on hand.)
RIB: Working thread, spiraled up the needle-supported foam abdomen.
THORAX: Light yellow synthetic dubbing.
WINGS: Clear 6 mil vinyl from a plastic bag.

COMMENTS: The Poly–Foam Spinner imitates a mayfly spinner. The foam is colored with a marking pen to mimic the natural.

Stalcup's Crane Fly, Tan
Shane Stalcup

HOOK: Standard dry fly, sizes 14 and 12.
THREAD: Tan 8/0 or 6/0.
ABDOMEN: A narrow strip of tan soft-foam.
LEGS: Monofilament, colored tan.
WINGS: Cream Z-lon, spent.
THORAX: Tan Furry Foam.
BACK and HEAD: Butt of the foam used for the abdomen.

NOTE: Black markings can be added. I found no patterns for Stalcup's Crane Fly other than this tan version, but it surely could be tied in other colors.

Sundown Spinner, Brown

Jan Weido

HOOK: Standard dry fly, sizes 18 to 14.
THREAD: Brown 8/0 or 6/0.
TAIL: Medium–blue–dun Micro Fibetts.
ABDOMEN: Rusty–brown dubbing.
BACK: Yellow or white soft–foam.
WINGS: White crinkled Z–lon.
THORAX: Rusty–brown dubbing.

COMMENTS: The foam back makes this fly more visible and more buoyant. I don't have a pattern for the Sundown Spinner other than this brown version, but it could certainly be tied in other colors.

Tan Foam Caddis

Dave Hughes

HOOK: Standard dry fly, sizes 18 to 10.
THREAD: Tan 8/0 or 6/0.
BODY: A strip of smokey–tan soft–foam. A rounded gape–long tab should extend over the bend; the remainder of the body is formed in two segments.
HACKLE: Brown, trimmed to a "V" beneath.
WING: Natural–tan deer hair.
HEAD: Trimmed wing butts.

Suspender Hatching Midge

John Goddard

HOOK: Short shank, down eye, sizes 18 to 12. (Wire thickness is not given in the pattern I found, but I'm guessing fine wire.)
THREAD: Dark 8/0.
PONTOON: A ball of Ethafoam in a pouch made from a nylon stocking. (I prefer to use a ball from injected polystyrene foam in the pouch.)
TAIL: White nylon filaments.
RIB: Fine, flat silver tinsel.
ABDOMEN: Black, brown, red, or green marabou or seal's fur.
THORAX: Brown–dyed turkey herl. (I used ostrich herl here.)

Yellow Foam Caddis

Dave Hughes

HOOK: Standard dry fly, sizes 18 to 10.
THREAD: Tan 8/0 or 6/0.
BODY: A strip of yellow soft–foam. A rounded gape–long tab should extend over the bend.
HACKLE: Light ginger, trimmed to a "V" beneath.
WING: Natural–tan deer hair.
HEAD: Trimmed wing butts.

INDEX

LEARN MORE ABOUT FLY FISHING AND FLY TYING WITH THESE BOOKS

If you are unable to find the books shown below at your local book store
or fly shop you can order direct from the publisher below.

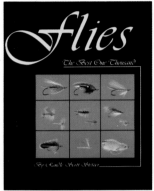

Flies: The Best One Thousand
Randy Stetzer
$24.95 (HB: $34.95)

Fly Tying Made Clear and Simple
Skip Morris
$19.95 (HB: $29.95)

The Art of Tying the Dry Fly
Skip Morris
$29.95 (HB:$39.95)

Curtis Creek Manifesto
Sheridan Anderson
$6.95

American Fly Tying Manual
Dave Hughes
$9.95

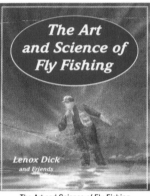

The Art and Science of Fly Fishing
Lenox Dick
$19.95

Western Hatches
Dave Hughes, Rick Hafele
$24.95

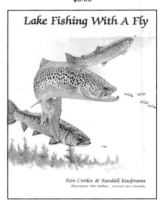

Lake Fishing with a Fly
Ron Cordes, Randall Kaufmann
$26.95

Advanced Fly Fishing for Steelhead
Deke Meyer
$24.95

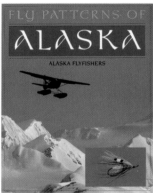

Fly Patterns of Alaska
Alaska Flyfishers
$19.95

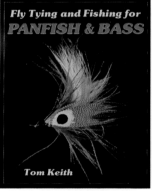

Fly Tying & Fishing for Panfish and Bass
Tom Keith
$19.95

Float Tube Fly Fishing
Deke Meyer
$11.95

VISA, MASTERCARD or AMERICAN EXPRESS ORDERS CALL TOLL FREE: 1-800-541-9498
(9-5 Pacific Standard Time)

Or Send Check or money order to:

Frank Amato Publications
Box 82112
Portland, Oregon 97282

(Please add $3.00 for shipping and handling)